This book is for my mother and father

Contents

Out in the Open

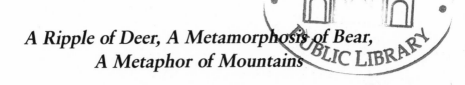

A Ripple of Deer, A Metamorphosis of Bear, A Metaphor of Mountains

I dream of mountains repeatedly,
running my fingers over maps where they spine
and cluster. Through valleys of rhododendron
and bear, wild pheasant and deer, I near them,
empty and still, leaning over my walking stick,
my breath easing out, a shrill whistle.
At night I stare at stars, cold and still, peaks
of invisible mountains in a sky steeply pitched.
As for crests, moraines and glaciers, icefalls,
seracs, cornices, spurs—they are psalms
of a wild solitude I am not brave enough to enter.

In the long journey to be other than I am,
I have struggled and not got far. Each day
l roam the fields, and I climb. I watch
from a shiver of aspen steep on a southern exposure
of cleared field. From the ridge rim of trees—
a ripple. A smooth shade of brown comes to merge
in the fern, gathering stillness and weight,
deer intent on the grass. I envy the deer.
Beyond them, the low mountains unroll. Clear nights,
I measure the cave depths of mountains
and their peaks—then in the hour between night
and dawn, the darkest, I dream into the mountain,

entering slim as a snake through cold soil
and stone. I wriggle down on my back, my soft parts
exposed, falling through caves rank as bear gut,
crooked as roots. *Accept who you are—*
of my labors the most naked and rigorous.
Mornings, I am what merges in the mists as I rise
from these depths, so attached to my ignorance,
I think I'm exalted, more rare than the seven
wise Hindu that ride in the constellation
we call the Great Bear. Then I envy the Bear.

Green Pepper

At the stem, at the breaking point,
a hard fray of cellulose narrows,
as if someone tied it off with a thread
and dipped it in iodine. Below
this point of harvest, the stem flares
to a sombrero of sorts at the base
of six green hills. This dream
of a green Southwest just fits
into my palm, planes that swell
to a finished surface of oil and wax
and silk. *Oasis, omphalos*—
the idea of water spills in.
My fingertips trace each yield
and slide of pepperskin north
and south, a surge into shadow
and line, shoulders and buttocks.
In the world of the pepper I'm plural,
polymorphous, perverse
as a play of light in the original
void.
          And you, so silent, abstracted . . .
if across the polished table I roll
this green pepper, if I call it
the philosopher's stone, will you
hold it to your ear and listen?
Inside there are whispers, whatever
you want to have whispered. Or else
the opposite—laws of energy,
a premise for desire so pure we shy
back to the more familiar.
You smile. You take the pepper,
with your thumbnail cut in it a window.
The flesh of the pepper is crisp.
Without tasting it, I know it is sweet.
And inside? A cluster beneath time
and surface, prior to it—the white
koan of seeds and stars.

Garlic

Up from the depths
of the raised bed of earth
the stalks lift thin banners,
green in the wind.
The roots clasp the soil,
with the reluctance of lovers
letting go. But the earth
breaks open, warm as biscuits,
and the pale bulbs, crusted
with earth crumbs, enter
for the first time
air. Braided, on green pigtails
lashed to the chickenwire gate
of the garden, each bulb
dries to a rustle,
weeks later, in my palm—
husky skins fine as rice paper,
veined like the leaf of a lily,
faintly varnished with gold.
Brittle papers that flake
when a thumb pries into
the cluster of cloves, prying
in and in, pinching the flesh
of a clove up under a nail—
and the odor! redolent,
a pungency in which pot roasts
and thick stews gather,
an aroma for eggplants and sesame
melding in a rich mystic kiss,
pure baba ganoush.
Let the feckless take it
odorless in capsules—
I simmer it in wine and tomatoes,
blend it with butter and basil,
lash the curved cloves
to a necklace I wear on my skin,
cold wolf-moon nights in the woods.
I stuff pillows with the skins,

rub the salad bowl of the lover's
body nightly with garlic,
breathe it out with the love cry,
let it rise, a nebula
into starry night skies . . .
for what if Dante were wrong
about paradise, the choirs
in their circular rows—what if
the celestial rose weren't petals
at all, but a commoner light,
a corona of cloves in their thin
garlic gowns, twisting up
into wicks that long to be lit,
and they are lit, flaming up
in the glory of God—
the God of the old myths
who leans over the fence
of the firmament, beyond pale
buds of new stars, leaning
our way, toward our own
common sod, sighing into it,
raising it, his breath
faintly garlic.

Swimming

I.

Instead, I conjure rivers,
the glide of the Susquehanna,
a heron unblinking on shore,
the whole length of me amber
and slippery in the turning river,
just one more ripple—
the Mississippi at Red Wing,
broad and generous, a promise—
and the Nile, the alluvial Nile,
in the delta a lotus unfolding.
Just now, I stretch out
in a river of salt and summer
phosphorus that kindles wet
flesh, our flesh, to a wander
of fire in dark water.
We glide into night so absolute
we barely surface, length
of me against length of you.
We travel great distances together,
letting our breath out slow.

II.

Remembering old lovers, I lean
into the lake, an interval
of water, a swing of sun—
by afternoon a surface so still
and clean and dark that clouds
and the sun too bright to see
reflect more clearly there.
There I skim into clouds
where lily and arrowhead root,
where sun is a moon. *I am*

is where *I'm not.*
Night deepens and fills
past its threshold of stars
and spills
beyond the far and near
horizons of my skin—
such spaciousness
in standstill and dissolution
that I feel quick
and light.

III.

I swim out alone at night.
The dark washes in,
stars spill, rivers burn.

Up there
In a river of wealth,
each star burns and falls
inward towards emptiness
I can't imagine—although
I can imagine giving
myself away,

giving myself away
constantly, not knowing if the gift
is greed—or generosity.

Karma

Try to believe this. Read
as if you are listening to
an ancient bamboo flute
whose wind is its own
echo, a bit of madness,
music chill and dark.
Dream yourself awake,
stretch, stamp your feet.
Life after life your name
is breath in the cold air,
a deep unknowing that gasps
at your ignorance and goes—
and here you are, a fiction
that swears to remember,
to touch one fragment
of your history. See now,
birds storm upriver,
gather in a wingspread,
one totemic black bird.
Think of those feathers,
how they would feel
stitched into a shawl,
pulled over my cold
naked breasts, silk and black.
Watch the falcon circle,
silently circle, right eye
the sun, left eye the moon.
The wings stir wind.
Skin feels it.

Skin feels it—just so,
when I see you, distant
or near, I surrender, bathe
in rose water, sweeten
my breasts. Naked as hands
wearing rings, I dance steps
I've learned from faded
temple walls, a rhythmic

limping. I slide my neck
sideways, paint my eyes.
Taste me, see through me
the deep blue of the universe,
bodiless and tender.
As the shadow of wings
blows over us, we lie down
in the oldest of lies, and
we are many, you and I—
we are the flute and the falcon,
the dancer and the lusty
embalmer who once took
my corpse, still fresh
from the marsh, and had it,
before he gutted and cleaned it,
before he washed the gray
mud from my hair.

Sensing the Enemy

Germany, 1972

Unravished, gathering gentians
in the shadows of low hills,
I want the dark blue earth to open.
My eyes still hurt from the glare,
my head from beer drunk down
too fast as bells rang across
the lake at Kloster Andechs,
where I asked and asked
what do I want to forget,
and answered *what do I not.*
As a child I was never allowed
to say *I hate.* But in this place,
a guest of history, I have never felt
as close to the war I was born in.
I have stood in the light
on bright gravel laid down fresh
between railroad ties. I have gone
to see where grief is mourned
and honored, needing to see
empty ovens, empty barracks,
clean floors, clean fields. All day
I have remembered myths—cycles
of rape and return and renewal.

I walk back to the house, foreign
and familiar, and I wait—
supper planned, a picnic in the orchard.
Inside an ordinary oven, bread bakes.
The lull of family life muses on,
children upstairs asleep with
their mother, their father gone off
to gather his parents for the evening.
Meeting others, we meet ourselves.
I forget that—I try to forget,
arranging my mood with wine, with
wildflowers limp on their stalks.
But words I have promised not to speak

sink into the blind side of my brain
and root. Once more, the myth returns,
the children vanish. The sun burns down.

Then dark, the family gathers
in the orchard. By this time, I had
intended to be drunk, to be sealed off
and cool, alone—for what can we talk
about? We talked, we smiled. Of course
we smiled, though now I remember
only the shock of seeing one old man,
and how the candles licked the air
clean, and a child danced
there on the wood table, naked
and smooth, each female tuck
of her skin, each fold perfect.
I close my eyes, look inward now,
and see steadily and whole the bowl
of plums on the table and that child
with dark, dancing eyes. She sits down
in the crook of her grandfather's arm,
looking into his face with delight—
and why not? Why not, I think.
His face is the face she has known
from her birth, a face that teases her
with plums and kisses, this man
shot down in the war I was born in,
his face a mask of fire-scar,
slick and blank—this man I will find
no less hard to forgive
than I find myself, or her.

In the Field

A low wind swings down the west ridge
over conifers and beech, thorn apple
and aspen, soundless
over wild lace and yarrow,
nightshade and thistle,
over haystalks and heal-all,
moving on the face of the mist—
at my feet a twist of bindweed,
on my arm a slant of mosquito,
my blood in its belly.
Shawls of white mist
rise sheer up the ridges,
a few rags left in the air
just over the low hills
and bottomland,
over a milkiness of blue
where the river loops
and coils, sliding by—
the great snake sheds
its skin once, and once
again, the river
rising ghostly in the air.
I watch a butterfly light
on a thistle, suckle, then float.
A mizzle of mountains nudges up.

I come into this solitude
where river and mountain and earth
meet a gradual sky,
where I live with the least
grass as it lifts
into the open, where mountains
float in the wind, eye-level
between thin stalks
of deer grass and hay—
into this interval of mist
and the wind's slow
tilt and touch, its blend with
the tree's own billow,

11

wind passing through burl
and branch and thorn,
through ways I have learned
to put an edge on time and space—
the mist rising of itself,
no striving, and I sense,
just before the slow release
of rain, coming to meet me in low
wind, as mysterious and distinct
as the scent of wild allium,
my own lift and well,
my wanting,
sweeter to me
than the fragrance of orchids.

Doing Nothing

I balance
on one foot, then the other,
reaching in for the pebbly berries
suspended on red whips and canes,
a lush clinging. On edge,
I reach in, the hone of a thorn
not unlike the whine
of mosquitoes beneath the leaves.
I pick my way in,
as if this discipline
has nothing to do with the moon
which last night opened
red, then paled
to the pale of a petal
in a still, black sky.
Slowly I pick my way in,
skillfully, a means that
has nothing to do with
doing harm
or with harvest.

For this moment, I forget
the pain that wants to
forget pain, and practice
touching lightly.
I watch my hands learn
their way past each
edge, each horizon,
lightly, touching
until between each berry
there is such space
I no longer have to hold
back, let go, or grasp.
Doing nothing, I
no longer wait for whole
other worlds to break open,
more beautiful than this one
whose wild darkness
stains my fingers,
my mouth, my tongue.

In the Desert

I.

Life is suffering, you say
lightly and turn your back,
adjust your pack and strike off.
The sparks fly upward,
crowding the emptiness we try
to fill with quarrel, haste
and wisdom, spires and prayers,
billboards, corridors, and beds.
We're in the desert together,
split apart, impoverished
no less than the spit-in-the-road
small towns, their tin roofs
bright as knife blades
and esperanza. Wings of shadow,
black, skim over red rock
crevices where agave and cactus,
sage and rosemary tether,
sea-level, in a collapsed basin
of salt and brittlebush rimmed
by mountains. We have read
the books on discipline
and freedom, the paradox of union—
and yet we neither speak nor hear
nor see nor touch each other.
I keep you ahead of me, in sight,
the road a margin of light
I can feel in my feet. I study
salt, creator and destroyer—
fill the print of my thumb
with salt, mark my forehead,
touch eyelids, tongue. I feel
body burn. I listen to the pain.

But who can I tell about nights
when the road spills out
from under my feet like water,
and fear is all I know,
the long fall to where words fail?

II.

Actually, the road is a rumple
in the sheets we've kicked
to the foot of the bed, the stars
a spill of seed, the moon
dark as earth, self-absorbed—
so that it stir not up nor awaken
love until it please. I touch
my body, not yours—a garden
locked, a fountain sealed,
a well of living water, mountain
of nard, aloes and calamus, saffron.
If you find my beloved, it is written,
tell him to imagine I've undressed
in the dark, the usual undoing,
an old clumsiness with buttons.
But that the close fit of skin,
the silk of muscle and sinew,
slip from me in the way of water
over rock. Light, I balance
on my bones, a loom pulled taut,
my spine stem and root.
Imagine that along that axis
of bone blossoms shiver and tilt.
For love is as strong as death,
though it will not be waked
until it please.

III.

I enter the solace of stone
and salt and bone, things
able to be as they are meant,
as I am not. *Don't go anywhere
without me. Let nothing happen
in the sky apart from me
or on the ground, in this world
or that world.* I don't say this
aloud. Shards of an old poem,
words jarred loose by walking,
they weren't meant for you,
walking with me, to hear.
Loose words do a simple magic—
they carry me where I cannot climb.
Like love, they make sense of
my longing.
         I think *wind*
and wait, stumbling in the light,
in the dark, and in the stammer
of the stars. Here dirt is red,
that cloud slate black, sky
white. Those who've walked here
before me, this silence is their
presence, this solitude their light
released. The sun rises into
itself, pale gold. The moon has
no desire to be described.
The stones do not ask to be holy.

IV.

On the steep road toward peaks
named for gods, named
for the nothing we know, not yet,
I find in hard sand, years old,
the word *listen,* the writing tool
a stone. I listen to the wind,
breathe in, choose one stone,
flat, flecked with mica,
a well of stars tucked smoothly
into rock of igneous origin,
dark feldspar washed down
an alluvial fan to this sinkhole
where we rise and fall. The edge
is what we have, salt margins
and stones that pulse like ancient
star charts. I tilt the stone,
light flaring on-off-on.
Listen. I say *canyon*
and hear only quiet glance off
centuries of schist, say *love*
and look past the horizon of personal
event, a gaze at distances
no words touch. I say *soul*
and wait. The stone begins to radiate,
to pray. *As thou wilt,*

what thou wilt, and when.

V.

Out of the wind
between close-textured rills
of bare shale we put down
for the night in a shallow ravine,
uneasy. Our counterparts,
the Twins, in perfect alignment
go on walking the river of fire
into the night. Orion shoots off
into emptiness, at random.
I listen for sidewinder, scorpion,
owl—dim movements
the intellect calls unknowable
and tries to know. Of nightwatch,
of bare waiting within an absence
of will this dark, I am incapable.
I hear whispers in the sand—
Consider the stars,
Like them anonymous and separate,
you are right to live in fear.
Why open your eyes at all?
I watch, as fear takes the shape
of a mountain still distant,
a ravine so near to the bone
it fits like muscle.

But then, in the silence
I hear you breathing, and I fit
my breath to yours. Not even
the mountain with its hood of cloud
is as impersonal, as full.
We breathe in and out with the stars,
in a universe whose darkness,
tangible and near, is the hidden place
where we are knit, woven fine.
Within us, this dark
broods, and breathes, and glows.

for David
Death Valley, 1987

After January 2

in memory of D.B.C.

In the library I read that our senses
are broken lights, blind guides.
I leave late, bundled for the cold,
breathing into my scarf to feel
my heat, measuring the long walk home
by streetlights and Orion. I concentrate
on the ice beneath my feet. And you,
whose sense of weight and light and heat
has yielded perhaps to the uncreated
light the mystics speak of—I don't know
I'm thinking of you until, struck
still by broken stars above the snow
and random houselights at the far rim
of a field and one tree in silhouette,
I say your name. I watch the syllables
change into visible breath, then vanish
where the moon, suspended east, will,
by morning. The road turns, taking me
suddenly into music, a minor key
that, but for the scrape of skates,
would be an easy grief. I cannot see
the skaters. Blue tarps against the wind
hang in taut strips along the rink,
releasing light in thin still verticals.
In the music, moving shadows flash on snow
outside the rink, where I am still
remembering your life and death—that is,
measuring what cannot be measured
by a flash of shadow on snow or by light
whose speed in emptier space is constant.
Love is a constant. I say your name
again, as if it might mean a destination,
and watch it cloud in the cold air
and float, just ahead of me, in the dark.

Keeping Still

Because I saw
my mother, tense or careless, snap the string of her necklace,
a spill of beads shooting round on the floor,

I thought stars were so—
beads that could therefore be gathered, in one place cupped,
the sky held in a single crystal.

What is as patient, as still
as that thought? I am listening to the traffic into Boston,
how it swells and falls, in the rain a sea rushing

past the dark house.
I have followed as far as I can, leaning out of my skin, past the red
shift of car lights, through the tidal dark clouds to a misting of stars,

reaching, wanting more.
Even the galaxies, restless, are rolling farther, each from each,
on the face of eternity moving, a sweep of bright cells

rinsed daily away.
My heart is not quiet. I want the faith that moves mountains.
I want the bright force that holds them still.

How can anyone stunned by the night's consolation of stars
dare say, "I have not seen what I want"—
and yet, I say it.

In Here

I.

On her breasts she rubbed
aloe and cast me off—
all the nouns of her body *past tense.*
But we shared a common universe,
the backyard, at whose gate
she stood when I returned—
How do you feel? Did you lose
the way? And the bed,
weekend mornings when she'd
murmur to me her childbed pain.
Childhood—a dark cloth
pulled over my head.

I travel back
to a backyard dark with
spring—hyacinths,
the wind, the willows
unknotting. Inside,
the door is clasped
with a porcelain bolt. I stir
hot milk and cereal in a pan.
She's propped in the window seat,
covered by blankets, her hair
thin and white. Before
I can spoon the food to her mouth,
she flicks her wrist
towards the window and says,

"It's not out there,
what we're afraid of." The moon
turns the floor to white water,
her bed and the shadow of her bed
to a boat. She pushes the spoon
aside and says to the room,
"It's in here."

II.

Out of the dark of her body
I emerged—it follows
that she will enter the dark
of my soul to die.
Afraid to stare into darkness
and see only dark, she gave
the womb, that slender pear,
an occult power—the Czar's
jeweled easter, a lush fig
with choirs of inward blooms,
a clockwatch on surface pleasure.
I shook my head—
"The body is a meditation shawl,"
I said. I couldn't look
her in the face and say
dark I prefer, nightgrass
and wind, the merge
of water and skin,
the mind's
unbounded membrane.

Outside,
the willow flings its green lines
to the wind and into the onrush of stars.
We listen to their silence,
pitched octaves down in the dark.
They do not tell how long
we will peel away the weave
of silk illusion, the lies
we wear—or if, face to face,
we can feel our way towards
light,
the fulcrum of our fear,
and there rest on balance—
naked,
self-forgetful.

for Kate

Last Rites, Recurring Dream

Even as I spoon you water
you do not wake.
I hold a full teaspoon
in an updraft of sun
through the window,
listening. An old question
ripples in—your original
face, the one before
you were born,
what was it?
No one answers, though your face
becomes less of a mask,
more of a perfect circle
merging nowhere, like dew
in the rage of sunrise.

You are more water than woman,
more fire than face,
neither my face nor anything
thought original
reflected beneath
the surface I peer into,
this water, this mirror
no longer
my chaos of old admirations,
gifts and accomplishments—
and what are these?

My eyes blur and remember.
Into that source
I spoon the tears of children
I thought you wanted me
to carry, and I wouldn't.
Into that source
I spoon the rain and sun
of all the journeys
you walked through,
shod with my feet.
I am singing you to sleep

in the dark,
as you used to sing me—
this song wordless,
risen up through
blind seams and fissures.

Whatever words I had saved
for this moment,
forgiveness, trust
go with you
into the wind that breathes
night and day alike,
one vision. I watch
and wait, sensing
in the shift of earth
to water, fire to air
new power.
Give me something to see,
I whisper, and ground opens.
Something to touch—
I stir the spoon in the glass,
watching spoon
and horizon dissolving,
the sharp rims of sun and moon
dissolving, not even
this glass
left to hold
not even that clear word
love—

only light.

for my mother

24

Out in the Open

in memory of R.H.B.M.

I.

The first signs of your illness I misread.
A change in character, I thought, annoyed
at the stubborn frequency of your needs.
Like a dog, you snapped at strangers.
Like a child, you had me up at night.
You'd want to go outside at any hour,
and you'd go, you'd stare at the moon
or the hard shell of snow left in the yard.
Sudden things far away seemed near.
You'd fix on them, stare off. Too fond,
you'd follow me about, insist some part
of your body towards mine, just touch.
Then the sheer fact of distance wore
you out. The tree in the open field
we'd walk to—too far. No memory
moved you from the quiet you slid into.
But when your skin seemed to loosen
and slur, when it slipped like an ill-
fitting cap down towards your eyes,
I called the doctors. They tested,
I bargained, made promises, pressed
down on hope as if hope were a seal
of eventual success. I held you, talked
nonsense, and sense, tried to tempt
you with food. I force-fed you, a tube
in the side of your slack jaw. Then
the shots, the intervals, the hours.
I'd go off to calm myself, come back
to find you'd managed to pull yourself
slowly over to the wall, find the corner,
a blind meeting, and stand there without
any sign of what it was you wanted,
as if you were pulled to an invisible
threshold, as of course you were.

II.

Before any of this, months before, an echo
of the unforeseen spun out of the blind spot
in my eye and made itself visible. I made
note of it, logged it in a journal of dreams,
more taken frankly by other things—a new
word, *piezoelectric,* and the fact that the bow
of a violin drawn deftly across the edge of
a metal plate shows the pattern of that note
in white powder on the surface of the metal.
That I magnified, forgetting the sand
that blew across the path of my dream, the dust
that insisted itself into all the open crevices
of my clothes and into my watch; forgetting
how I called you to me, hoarse, wanting
you to stay, at the same time distracted
by a replica of bird, long-legged and blue,
by shells and other artful surfaces that took
my fancy, ignoring the point of steep descent,
the black hole we stood at the edge of—
a dense space where night felt like justice,
and more—the sense that the bird of the dream
had that emptiness for its nest.

III.

Today, putting to rights your things,
fully aware of the elsewhere that sinks
through the edges of everything I touch,
I recall that dream, in the mood for echoes.
The doorbell rings, and I open to a kid
up the street who loved you, too. Unsteady
on his roller skates, he's brought down
an envelope sealed tight. He touches
the threshold for balance, letting air out
shy between the spaces of his teeth.
The note says everything simply and right,
if transformed by the code of his spelling.
You he's drawn underneath the tree in the open
field, beneath a squat yellow sun and a deft
V of birds drawn into a distant vanishing
point beyond paper. He watches me read
and laugh through tears and praise his art—
but neither of us, I think, can think to see
the dark blue silhouette of bird he's put
in the branches of the tree, long-legged,
for what it is. We hug, he skates off
on the shifting winter sand of the road,
and for one brief moment, watching him go,
I see everything out in the open—not knowing
which to bless more—your life, life itself,
or the patterns, blind in time, we learn to see.

In the Woods

Between dreams, desperate,
I stare at the sun's slow
swing, a hypnotist's crystal.
Tell all the truth, it says,
tell it slant. How else,
walking lightly on the earth,
can I tell it? Through
jigsaws of shagbark and briar
I map paths with my eyes,
sudden openings and arches,
then weave through. Of the Tao
it is written—*Look,*
you can't see it. So here I am
looking, hooking east with
the brook, sun now a rickrack
of light on bare branches,
a screen of white silk on the sky.
From above it's not bright.
From below it's not dark.
Where then is the gate to its mystery?

I lie down in the leaves by the brook,
I fill with dark sky. And the trees—
seen from a slant, what are they
but slashes of reed, the loose
weave of a basket or cradle.
Rocking deeper asleep,
I walk the high ridges.
Granite ledges jut out into air.
Still as centuries, pale lichens
bloom, here on the stones,
the whole planet a prayer wheel.
I sit down in this thought,
unwinding myself to a thread,
a bit of mooring left by a web
when the wind's torn through.
Briar rock blossom brook—
the Tao I can name is not
the eternal Tao. But here I am,

lightly bound to this life—
and the mystery I look for,
I'll call it the new moon,
a darkness within darkness.
Watch it rise.

Double Vision

Tonight I slip into bed
and read Eckhart, how he
floats in the river and fount
of the Godhead, no one
to question where he is
going, what he is doing.
Everything in the Godhead
is one—and of that
there is nothing to be said.
Blessed indeed are the pure
in heart for they shall see
each night what I cannot—
elsewhere, perhaps still
in Goerlitz, light falls
on a burnished pewter plate,
and a shoemaker spills
inward, by the holiest
abstraction held, so that
outside afterward
grass and trees and wind
reflect that light.
I watch the moon fill,
changing earth to water,
to clouds the mountains
rising in the sky.
Just visible outside,
the shagbark glows—
once, in the room
I turned startled towards
a sudden tone and saw,
bright as a majolica plate,
suspended on nothing,
by nothing,
a disk of light,
neither sun nor moon.
In the room, no other
thing appeared
or brightened, darkened
or lessened. Then it went

out like a spark. Of God,
the idea of God as visible
as salt in water—to speak
of God I wasn't mad enough,
still enough, called.
That night I went
back to my book.
The wine I drank down fast.

Lemons: A Symposium

The morning's rising, red and gold,
and here I am, *soror mystica,* scribe
of the kitchen sink—mucking about
for seeds in the catch of the drain.
I want to check my sources, to footnote
De Circulo Physico Quadrato
with fact. I know the Latin for *gold,*
the Hebrew for *light* trace back
to a common root. I've read
that countless revolutions of the sun
have spun about the earth
threads of gold, a net not even night
unravels. If the language of light
is what I look for,

                  this lemon seed,
sleek and visible, more humble,
will have to do. I tamp it into
a pot of soil black as coffee,
soak it wet. Already in the hush
of the earth, I hear wind rising,
wind in the leaves of a lemon tree,
gold rush—

            and here it is,
as surely as energy follows thought,
the lemon of all lemons, secure
in its own skin, a replica
of its seed in the sweep of its line,
swelled and full. The stem end,
puckered, resembles a nursing
mother's nipple. Its topknot
peaks like the shikhara of a buddha,
the crown chakra aloft in light.
Before its silence, I put my hand
over my mouth and swear to fret
and cavil no more.

               No sooner said,
the same lemon I have called
elixir of union, fountain of light,
essence of water and flame

woven tight—quickly I ransack
for use, a garnish with parsley
for fish, a wedge on a tiny fork.
I remember pitchers of lemonade,
summer's hot breeze on the porch,
sweat on the glasses.
                    I remember
lemon chess pies so tart we pursed
our lips. Not to mention remedies,
the alchemies cool and stringent—
lemons for itching, for fever, flu.
We rinse our skin white, our hair
bright with a savor of lemons,
make a pomander of lemon and cloves
for the closet—what we won't do
with an airglow of lemon, the wet
aurora of its fruit. How we fret.

for my father

Cactus Blooms

Out of flat green stems
as jointed as the limbs
of salty crustaceans,
pale buds one by one
swell and flush. Hour
by hour the air around
them deepens, a stellium
of red suns rising over
shorelines of dark magenta.
If my senses were other
than they are, I might
hear the horn concertos
these blooms baroquely
unfold, might see
the uprush of spirit
in a fire of cinnabar
and summer, might hear
the wind sweep through
prayer flags, translating
their silences down sheer
mountain ridges, plains
and rivers. But I am
what I am, a woman
at a standstill who keeps
on, who keeps on
with images that lead
her eye off to strange
altars—this bloom
the ruff of a fire god
too holy to be touched.
And then I touch it. I tap
gently, once, and the nectar
rolls onto my finger.
I taste it, just this much—
and then I let it be.

for Jean

Beginner's Mind

When I begin to see
only what I've said—
my breath in the air
a snow of blind
keyholes and braille—
I let the dogs loose
in the field, and we run.
In the dimness of trees
by the wall, they chase
memories of squirrels.
I follow the wind until
out of breath
I crouch down in blank
snow, glad of the burn
of cold air in the west,
the border of trees
black and still.
Even now the magnolia
has buds, brushtips
of branches that lift
into the open.
Overhead, slate blue,
clouds swift along east.
I wait until stars
come into the blue—
then the black
never nowhere a child
gets quietly lost in.
I race the wind home.
In the kitchen new buds
of narcissus,
paperwhites unseasonal
in their bowl of stones
on the sill, have opened.
But my eye comes to rest
on a glass cup, cobalt blue,
which once, a child,
I named first when I named

what around me in the room
was living. I lift the glass,
turn it slowly in the light,
its whole body full of light.
Suddenly I hold everything
I know, myself most of all,
in question.

Making Salad

after Eihei Dogen

I rub the dark hollow of the bowl
with garlic, near to the fire enough
so that fire reflects on the wood,
a reverie that holds emptiness
in high regard. I enter the complete
absence of any indicative event,
following the swirl of the grain,
following zero formal and immanent
in the wood, bringing right to
the surface of the bowl the nothing
out of which nothing springs.

I turn open the window above the sink
and see fire, reflected on the glass,
spring and catch on a branch a light
wind tosses about. Here or there,
between new leaves the Pleiades,
like jewels in the pleromatic lotus,
flash. I watch the leaves swirl
and part, gathering light fresh
from Gemini, ten millennia away, fresh
from Sirius—holding each burning
leaf, each jewel within whatever light
a speck of conscious mind can make,
unshadowed by reflection or design,

impartial. Out the tap, from a source
three hundred feet down, so close
I feel the shudder in the earth, water
spills over my hands, over the scallions
still bound in a bunch from the store.
I had thought to make salad, each element
cut to precision, tossed at random
in the turning bowl. Now I lay the knife
aside. I consider the scallions. I consider
the invisible field. Emptiness is bound
to bloom—the whole earth, a single flower.

Things Unseen

Ramakrishna crosses a paddy field
holding a large bowl of rice,
sees—flying in a flock
against black clouds—
white cranes. Struck,
he falls into the field, rice
everywhere, scattered.

Van Gogh—in a cedar field
broods, watches near
stars and their motions
go counterclockwise, storms
that whirl into hot roses—
open at the center, hive yellow,
no more astral than the leap
and quiver of his flesh.

The evidence of things unseen
adds up/comes down to us
as rice and roses.
What's left of ecstasy spurls
into the visible, into nights
when the sound of the river meets
the sea. You close the door,
leaving light inside—down

the sloped sky, a spill of milk
no one sifts for myth
or magnitude or clock. You feel
open space spread wide between
your cells—the stars' breath
this instant. You do not
hesitate to pluck an empty
twig. The blossom's there.

Sky hovers and springs, the stars
flung—everywhere rice,
everywhere pollen and petals,
sparks of meteors, snowballs,
fresh syllables— the bowl

unbroken. The bowl still full—
Li Po drinks with a recluse,
face to face, among the mountains.

for Jacqueline

What Rings Through

In Zagorsk I walk where stones
are worn, more than ever in love
with the holy world of words,
around me an icon screen of sun
and the linden's fragrant shade,
overhead a mystic harvest, onions
blue and gold.
                    I wait for sudden
vision, try to think what I feel
watching the float of a monk's
black skirt over stone, his face,
holy or not, hidden. I envy
the workers in the courtyard
laying stone, slowly thinking
with their fingers.
                    Though I try
several questions in Russian,
I can't speak. I become a rough
translation, a thought in two
languages, no thought. Light falls
in the shift between *I* and *Я*,
as light will in a break between
old stones in a wall.
                    I breathe in
the sun and listen, blind
to the onions of noon blue
and midnight stars, drawn instead
by the shuffle of feet on stone,
by bells and the ringing-through
of bells, that afterthought of sound
at rest in silence.
                    I hear
my constant, own contradiction,
a ringing-through of all I've said
or willed, and go into the church
of St. Sergius—a sudden shock
of darkness, a place of women,
their bodies in singular reverence.

I close my eyes, hold fast, hold in
my breath.
        Here, there are words
to trace in a musk of music
on my skin, a Cyrillic hypnosis
of words that tease me beyond
translation, correctly strange.
In that quiet, I am quiet. And God—
whatever God is,
            God is unseen,
only sensed in a shift of light,
unspoken, a ringing-through of voices
that have sped over centuries
of snow on fire with sun, blowing in
here to hover in a darkness
black as earth.
            I am standing
in the dark with a woman whose face
is as calm as an icon, her eyes
blind, her head covered with the common
black cloth on which bloom roses,
fire and thorn—a simple woman,
concrete and still. She is smiling—
and that is my vision.

Stalking the Light

I.

Where ridge falls away to thicket
and brook borders field,
I settle into a still hunt,
heavy with rest-energy,
at one with the unshaken grace
of stone. However still, I may not
win a glimpse of the shy
habitual deer, the spotted thrush,
the owl, nor be enough within
the company of things, withdrawn
to a common depth, so that I know
the halsing and singular solace
of being equivalent and simple.
Restless, my way is to rise
and go into the stand of light
between the stand of trees,
without knowing what draws me
there, within the light,
stalking it, my own light hidden.

II.

But for the moment I sit, recalling
one gold-toned photograph
of Black Belly, Cheyenne—her face
a map of ten thousand journeys.
She worked in the sun,
hard work, long concentration—
of the kind no one praises
or would think to praise,
work too necessary, too close
to the body's survival, a discipline
that's made her skin craze.
I study her burning solitude,
her disregard for pain,

and try not to compare.
If there are wordless histories
we share, I let them come
to common focus in a split seed,
beech or oak—by root descending,
stalk ascending, riven.

III.

Whether I stalk or still hunt
or simply walk, I take with me
these guides—old Black Belly,
whose steps are slow,
and the split seed that opened
for me the root of *glad*
and *glade*, a shimmering space
that spills here and there
among the trees. I also call
to mind a young Vietnamese
who walked into my life
with a sunflower on its long stalk
as his walking stick, who taught me
to count and to breathe
so that within each step a fresh
breeze rose. I'd go alone,
but my solitude spins me
in circles—I read compass
and moss and the wind all wrong.
Rivers seem to flow backwards,
known outcroppings fade. I lose
my bearings, pressing into
the illusion of getting there—
somewhere, anywhere—
on the long way up the tangled
ridge toward sun and open rock.

IV.

Walking, I dream of that pure land,
Ladakh, bare rock mountains,

gravel slopes, bare sandy plains
where silence and light conjoin,
and all things are backlit
by the infinite—Kangri La,
a stupa, a sandal tree, apricots
spread on a flat roof to dry,
a stone—things justly placed
in a mandala imagined for so many
centuries, it's there. There,
a quiet shift of light moves
mountains. There, I lay
all my books into the stream
that flows down from the mountain
and watch words rinsed of their
griefs and hungers. I listen
for the still small voice
that follows windstorm and fire—
a voice before whose whisper I cover
my face in a mantle, impersonal,
unable to fear devastation—
broken houses, blackened fields,
the forest reduced to an oak
whose holy seed is its stump,
the city down to its last, a child
whose seed is a crooked helix,
a source from which no energy
spills, that bleak singularity
where light, as we know it, ends.

V.

The wind makes the sound of hours
in the trees, a flash of sun
between hemlock and beech
the only blaze that marks
the lower rise. Higher up—
a flare of mica, ribs of birch,
a skin of water over rock.
I collect the names of the lowly,
my companions—self-heal,
hobblebush, fireweed, frail sedge—

flowers close to green, colors
that do not carry, mountain
surfaces that resemble the worn
weave of prayer rugs.
When the wind comes at me
blindside, I give up the search
for a home here, become
properly alone. Walking,
I push up from the earth
and feel my weight. Mass
after mass, the mountains heave,
holding firm. Somewhere,
hidden by all this light,
part of it, the planets
fall freely, traveling as straight
as they can through curved space.
At the core of what I am,
in that sacred space, light
does its work, as it will
without my consent
or blessing—and better so.
I climb, and the sun climbs,
at midday abundant, brief.

In the Mountains

In the mountains, I listen—
tracing the way
mountains arch through
air without effort,
without artifice. Out here
I can almost understand
how mountains are
words said
at a height—actual
sound made manifest
as silence, a summons
I try to imitate
setting these words down,
keeping low in the power.

This morning I give
whatever slender means
I am—an eye without
self-pity, without anger—
to the lift of sun and mist
across the surface
of what seems to be repose,
to the mountains,
to the great standing still
of thought
to whose center I feel
myself drawn.

Around me, peak after peak
the mountains circle,
the air thin and clear.
Not one leans out of itself
into next week's sun.
Not one sinks
in my regard,
diminished to a stone
I can pocket
or keep in a bowl
with the rocks I collect
on the ridges as I walk.

In this pause, I ask to be turned,
circling the mountains
on a scale of wind and sun,
until I am once more
down on my knees at the lowest
rise, where the spring is,
listening, able to tell—
as the mountains flow
without flowing,
as the spring deepens
and stills
beneath its own precise
ripples and rills—
who breathes, who abides,
who rises, standing still.

Journeys

I.

Because you're leaving home,
ready to test your solitude
and courage, ready to travel
distances and stand right
at the edge of the unknown—
and because you've taken
free passage into the wind,
without rites, without ritual,
I've been remembering seekers,
nomads—Basho on the narrow
road to the deep north, his own
shadow frozen to his horse.
He found room to celebrate
bush clover, pampas, the moon,
and carried temple silences
within him, glad in the occasional
wind in dark cedars, his ear
on rice planting songs, or
a cricket that sounded inside
a discarded helmet. From these
he made syllables delicate
as dew, a cameo of moments.
Or Lady Wen-Chi of China,
taken by ruffian Mongols
from her home of gauze windows,
green patios, and mirrors
to the sky's edge, to a wild
land beneath the river of stars
where migrations of geese
steered away from messages
her flute would send home.
She learned to clean her hair
with mutton fat, to count time
by the year-star, to wait
to understand nights and days
she would write down once back
in the ruined house—where

she lit candles in the ashes,
rinsed her jade, and returned
to daily rituals that said
who she was.

We are all travelers,
I remind myself, sojourners
in a foreign land—and a phrase
comes back to me from a tale
of rugs that nomads weave
on the narrow looms they fold
and travel with, wandering
what worlds there are to know—
a shimmering phrase
meant for rugs of nine colors,
finely knotted, with designs
of birds and flowers, suns
and moons. This small amulet,
this phrase I would give you
to take with you as you go,
this prayer—that you may have
windows to walk on.

II.

Think with me of windows,
those at home, clear panels
that look out on oak and beech,
and down on the quiet pond,
red-winged birds in the rushes,
a fleet of clouds and geese
in the unrippled water—
think of the arc of the moon
rising in the east window,
rolling down the west, and let
yourself, one night too beautiful
to sleep, the house hushed,
open those windows
into your whole life, behind
you and ahead. You will feel
your thoughts settle down

to one fine thread
unspooling. That thread
is the road you walk on—
you are the road, where it opens,
where it ends. Know
what you want, and taking up
the thread, as you go tie
knots of shadow, sun
and moon, taproot and hawk
on the wing, mist and stone,
thorn and flower, rain
in the deep ravine.
Within you, like ancient rugs
on wide temple floors,
there are patterns to weave by,
visions that lie still
and will not rise and fall
with each gust of desire
or fear, if you trust them.
Trust them—
             this advice,
if that's what it is,
I make from what I have on hand—
a book on rugs that are windows;
small clarities, hard won;
and a compassion you don't know
about just yet. Basho heard
in the silence of a flower
bells. Once home, Wen-Chi
remembered the turning patterns
of geese and stars. The world
has an order beyond our own—
we travel in a wheel of sparks
that fly outward from the center,
our sun one of these.
As you go, remember the windows,
how sun follows moon—at the outset
darkness, in darkness blessing,
the sun rising—great harvest.
All goes well.

for Joshua and Megan

Rings of Fire

I.

Deer in the field, a lucid morning,
no mist—the air clean, brisk
after last night's thick rain.
Uphill, apples hang in an eddy
of wind, dawn red, august gold.
Summer in the field, for us,
is closing—you left quickly
and went in town to buy new locks.
I relax into the detail of the day,
packing china, foodstuff, books—
housework as meditation, housework
as power—I the very wry
and proper instrument to lead
us all from chaos. Efficient,
I summon St. John, who saw arise
new heaven and new earth. I bow
to Brother Lawrence, Paracelsus,
and the physicist who put God
where God belongs,
in the detail of the universe—
albeit a universe randomly
holy, discontinuous, unevenly
plucky with photons and stars,
spontaneous. In no time
I'm in free fall,
weightless in the rift
between what I am and what I know.
As above, so below. I empty
shelves, fill boxes, label,
and flee outside, into the field
of goldenrod and fern and hay
where, invisibly, updrafts rise—
spinning rushes of wordless ascent
hawks open their wings to—
into the silence.

II.

We have seen the field in full moon
and no wind—a perfect
equilibrium, soul at a standstill,
white as milk—and felt
indifferent. We've seen the field
rise like an ocean that's swelled
all night to get here—and continued
yesterday's arguments, bitter
and wrong. Just once I saw a book
left outside in the field,
spilled open by wind,
pages beating into wings
until high up, higher,
absorbed by the shining of the sky—
I could see through book and bird,
a bit of gold aloft in gold,
hard to find. So would I burn.
So would you.

III.

The crickets chant "chi" and "chi"
and circulate the light—
invisible Chinese sages. I smile.
Lower down on the slope, in grass
like new spring chives, I measure
the distance to the mountains,
space across which a message
might fly—come home.
Sun's hot on my jeans, my sweater,
and my face when I lift it
to the sun. I'm in sunfall—
a wind of light that sweeps
downhill as the clouds race,
touching first the crest,
the apples, hawthorn,
hayheads, sweet grass,
yarrow, this body and beyond—

a sweep of shade, then sun,
in so swift an alternation
that I think I can—I can—
have nothing, want nothing,
and be glad.

IV.

Into this clarity of light,
into this ring of fire in the field
you come—here almost too magically—
and join me in light so bright
it must approximate (so I've read)
the last of the visions released
by one who's dying—space
like light rinsed clean after long
hard rain, a sense of sun
redoubled. But when you touch me,
the book of the future closes.
Here there is light and shadow,
hawk and wind, my nipples,
your tongue, apples, aspen,
mountain, stalk, bare skin,
the plane and sweep of bodies
moved to touch and hold.
Love is clearer than thought,
as strong as air and fire,
as the ocean of wind in the trees,
as sun in the strong green grass.

V.

From here there is no milkiness
in the mountains, neither on the ridges
nor in the field. The valley
is explicit, frankly green,
the line of the far hills and mountains
precise—they are where they are,
what they are. At that horizon

I see how everything stops, full
and clear, beyond it nowhere to go
just now. No mountain to cross,
no river, no road. Turning home,
we're home already, at rest in
the visible. I see this field,
this widening circle of sun,
light so bold I cannot see
the subtle world that exceeds it
and enfolds—once,
in a dream the blue sky opened
wide, and night with its other
million suns spilled through.
Even now, they are here.
When we touch, joining silences,
we travel in their light—
with earth to write our words on,
water to soothe, fire to quicken.
The wind breathes light
into our bones—turning stars
into power we can touch, impulse
we can follow or tell, teaching love—
for that is what we are.

Notes to the Poems

"In the Desert," III: "Don't go anywhere without me" and the following lines in italics are from "In the Arc of the Mallet," in *Open Secret: Versions of Rumi,* translated by John Moyne and Coleman Barks.

"In the Desert," IV: "As thou wilt . . ." is a paraphrase of a prayer by Thomas a Kempis.

"What Rings Through": Я is the first-person pronoun in the Russian language, pronounced *ya*.

"Stalking the Light": "halsing and singular solace" is from Richard Rolle, *The Fire of Love. Halsing* is an archaic word that means "embracing."